ALTAR MINISTRY HANDBOOK

A Guide for Altar Workers

R. L. Bowen, Th.D.

Altar Ministry Handbook
A Guide for Altar Workers
by R. L. Bowen, Th.D.

Printed in the United States of America

ISBN 978-1-60477-917-2

www.xulonpress.com

ACKNOWLEDGMENTS

There are many who directly or indirectly have contributed or influenced this work. I wish to express my gratitude to each of them for their inspiration and patience in working with me to accomplish what I consider to be a very useful tool for the Body of Christ.

To my precious wife and daughter you continually show your unending love and support for my work. Your encouragement has spurred me on to complete this work and to press on to complete what has been assigned to me.

To Judy Belmontes for your wisdom in writing and your editorial skills, I am ever grateful. You have been an inspiration and personal support to me. Your gentle way of encouraging me to change things for the better is very much appreciated.

For Barry Muenkel whose knowledge has made this project flow more easily. Your commitment to excellence is a delight and you willingness to assist me on this project is truly refreshing.

To Tony Vento who first peaked my interest thinking about the need for such a work.

Most of all I thank the precious Lord Jesus Christ in my life, without Him this work would never have been written. You took a broken man and made something from nothing and for that I will be forever grateful and thankful for your mercy and your grace in my life.

To every reader, my prayer is that this book will enable you to better lead others to a personal relationship with our Lord Jesus Christ.

INTRODUCTION

Years ago when we started New Song Christian Fellowship Church, I looked for a manual to use to teach altar workers the appropriate way to minister to those that are seeking. While there may be some works on the market, I was not able to find anything that I felt appropriate. In observing others as they ministered to those in need it became increasingly aware that there was a great need for a work such as this one.

The focus is to make the work helpful but not cumbersome, insightful but not boring, Word based and not someone's idea or theory. I believe this manual does those things in a manner that enables both small churches and large ministries to benefit from this work.

While all churches may not use all of the information in this book it will provide a resource that will enable that church to lead those that are seeking into a closer walk with our Lord Jesus Christ.

We as Christian leaders must get back to the Bible and its teaching. Far too long we have watered down or made too easy the commitment of becoming a Christian. When the Holy Spirit reaches down and convicts an individual to turn to Him, we must be ready to perform our responsibility and lead that person soundly to Christ, on into baptism and beyond.

This is a manual to be carried and used by altar workers for the purpose of pointing people to Christ and growing into a deeper relationship with Him.

CONTENTS

CHAPTER 1

The Purpose of Altar Ministry

Altar ministry serves as a critical link for those seeking answers to life's tough questions and for those who desire a meaningful life-change. It is a source of encouragement, a place of prayer support, and a bridge that responds to an individual's specific needs. Altar ministry is essential if effective guidance is to take place in your church services. Many people are searching for truth. It is both the privilege and responsibility of the Altar Ministry Worker to be very sensitive to the person that is before you. Wrong counsel may be worse than no counsel. The Word of God has the answer and it is necessary that the Altar Ministry Worker be familiar with the Word of God enough to be able to give Biblically sound guidance. It must be the desire of the Altar Ministry Worker to provide much needed help and direction in a world of chaos and misdirection. Without capable and effective guidance, non-biblical theories creep in and often the spiritual direction is skewed away from a vibrant, victorious personal relationship with Jesus Christ. Our ultimate goal as an Altar Ministry Worker is to guide people to Jesus.

The Strategy of Altar Ministry

There should be an Altar Ministry Team for each church service. However, depending on the size of your church or the expected number of altar call respondents, one or more Altar Ministry Teams may need to be available. The Altar Ministry Team diagram that is depicted in this book features two teams and specifies the number of members on each team, each position title as well as the order of leadership within each team. The Altar Ministry Team follows the overall direction of the Senior Pastor in ministering to those responding to the altar call. An information card, referred to in this book as a "Follow- up Card" is also a part of the altar ministry process (*see Appendix B*). The Altar Ministry Worker makes sure that a follow-up card is completed for each person/couple responding at the altar. The information on this card is given to the Altar Ministry Team Leader who provides this information to the Senior Pastor. The Altar Ministry Director then arranges additional follow-up with the altar call respondent. Generally, the best person to do the follow-up is the Altar Ministry worker who initially spoke with the individual desiring assistance. Follow-up is absolutely critical to the growth and development of the individual requesting assistance. An individual that is left without follow-up from Altar Ministry often times does not understand and can become discouraged not knowing what to do or what direction to take. Altar ministry is a continual process of beginning discipleship to assisting the spiritual conversion, growth and development of lost and troubled souls. This strategy is explained in detail in the following pages.

The Benefits of Altar Ministry

Altar ministry team members respond to an individual at a time of heightened awareness and receptivity to God's voice. Providing encouragement and prayer at this pivotal time assists the individual responding to the altar call in making a powerful personal connection with God. The Altar Ministry Worker is key in connecting the person to a ministry within the church, which provides opportunity for ongoing and long-term spiritual growth in the life of the individual responding to the altar call, i.e., Men's Group, Women's Group, or other programs offered by your church. Encouraging the person to become involved in areas of interest will help that person to be rooted and grounded in your church. As a result, they will become a part of the growth of your church with a feeling of belonging. The Altar Ministry Worker may introduce the individual to one or several department areas in order for the individual to feel welcome, significant and useful. This will happen as the individual grows and matures in their personal walk with the Lord Jesus. However, the Altar Ministry Worker should never "promise" an individual a specific place to volunteer in your church. Care must be taken and procedures followed in order that all church attendees are protected. We are admonished to "know those that labor amongst us". Be confident that you know and understand your church's policies with regard to volunteers before placement is suggested.

CHAPTER 2

Altar Ministry Team Format Diagram

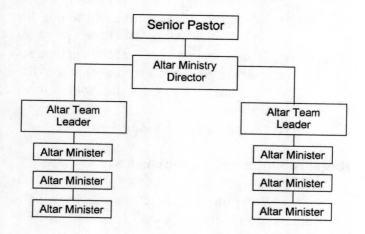

As stated previously, there should be one or more Altar Ministry Teams at every service depending on the size of your church. Each team is comprised of a team leader, co-leader and up to five altar ministers. During special events, all teams may need to be available to serve for optimum results. The responsibilities or position descriptions for each member of an Altar Ministry Team are detailed on the following pages.

Altar Ministry Director Position Description

Title: Altar Ministry Director

Reports to: Senior Pastor

Summary: The Altar Ministry Director oversees the activities of the Altar Workers in all church services, including special event services, provides training for potential Altar Workers, provides information and offers encouragement to those serving on the Altar Ministry Team. Ensures follow up.

Authority: Appointed by Senior Pastor

Responsibilities and Requirements:

- The Altar Ministry Director shall be a born again, spirit-filled, water baptized, mature member of your church
- The Altar Ministry Director shall regularly participate in church services
- The Altar Ministry Director shall offer regular training sessions and timely information to the

Altar Ministry Team members and to those with potential for Altar Ministry

- The Altar Ministry Director will submit the names of potential Altar Ministry Team members to the Senior Pastor for approval
- The Altar Ministry Director will monitor the follow-up process of the Altar Ministry in coordination with the Senior Pastor
- The Altar Ministry Director shall work in a cooperative manner with the pastoral staff, other ministry directors and the support staff of your church
- The Altar Ministry Director will provide leadership that is in harmony with the vision, values and virtues of your church
- The Altar Ministry Director shall meet all requirements as specified above

The Altar Ministry Director will be a resource person and mentor to the Altar Ministry team leaders and team members. This is a servant position and must be seen as such. The ability to discern spiritual needs and direct people appropriately is absolutely necessary for the person serving as Altar Ministry Director.

Term of Office: One-year term. The term can be renewed for consecutive years. The Altar Ministry Director serves at the discretion of the Senior Pastor.

Altar Ministry Team Leader Position Description

Title: Altar Ministry Team Leader*

Reports to: Altar Ministry Director

Summary: The Altar Ministry Team Leader coordinates the activities of the Altar Ministry Workers in their assignments, ensuring that each individual responding to the altar call receives effective ministry.

Responsibilities and Requirements:

- The Altar Team Leader shall be a born again, spirit-filled, water baptized member of your church
- The Altar Team Leader shall regularly participate in church services
- The Altar Team Leader assists the various team members by directing team members to those individuals needing altar ministry, making sure follow-up cards are completed for each respondent to the altar call, and collecting the follow-up cards at the close of the service
- The Altar Ministry Team Leader is expected to be in attendance at their assigned service. When the Altar Ministry Team Leader must miss attending a service, the Altar Team Leader is expected to contact the Altar Ministry Team

Director <u>prior</u> to the service and make the necessary arrangements to assure that their responsibilities will be covered

- The Altar Team Leader will assist in all Altar Ministry training sessions
- The Altar Team Leader shall work in a cooperative manner with the pastoral staff, other ministry directors, and the support staff of your church
- The Altar Team Leader will provide leadership that is in harmony with the vision, values, and virtues of your church
- The Altar Team Leader shall meet all the requirements as specified above

The Altar Ministry Team Leader will be a resource person and mentor to the Altar Ministry Worker. This is a servant position and must be seen as such. The ability to discern spiritual needs and direct people appropriately is absolutely necessary for the person serving as Altar Ministry Team Leader. The Altar Ministry Team Leader serves at the recommendation of the Altar Ministry Director and approval by the Senior Pastor.

Term of Office: One-year term. The term can be renewed for consecutive years at the discretion of the Senior Pastor.

* *In smaller churches, there may be no need for this position*

Altar Ministry Team Member Position Description

Title: Altar Minister

Reports to: Altar Ministry Team Leader*

Summary: The Altar Minister serves as a facilitator of prayer and follow-up to those responding to an altar call during church services, special events or outreaches.

Responsibility and Requirements:

- The Altar Minister shall be a born again, spirit-filled, water baptized member of your church
- The Altar Minister shall regularly participate in church services
- The Altar Minister shall have an understanding of spiritual gifts, and be in agreement with the doctrines and practices of your church
- The Altar Minister is expected to be in attendance at each assigned service. When the Altar Minister must miss attending a service, the Altar Minister is expected to contact the Altar Ministry Team Leader or Director prior to the service and make the necessary arrangements to assure that their responsibilities will be covered
- The Altar Minister is to provide assistance that is consistent with Altar Ministry Guidelines

- The Altar Minister will attend all Altar Ministry training sessions
- The Altar Minister shall work in a cooperative manner with the pastoral staff, other ministry directors and the support staff of your church
- The Altar Minister will provide leadership that is in harmony with the vision, values and virtues of your church
- The Altar Minister shall meet all the requirements as specified above

Term of Office: One-year term. The term can be renewed for consecutive years. This individual is appointed by the Altar Ministry Director and approved by the Senior Pastor.

* In smaller churches, if there is no Altar Minister Team Leader, this individual reports to the Altar Minister Director

CHAPTER 3

Standards for Service

The Biblical principles of service require that time and energy are given because of love for God and people. As a servant of God within your community, the Altar Ministry Worker will endeavor to relate to fellow workers in a loving and caring manner consistent with Scriptural teaching. In light of this foundation of service, the Altar Ministry Worker willingly accepts the following requirements for service in this church family:

In The Area of My Spiritual Life:
I recognize that I am a new creation in Jesus Christ and will do my utmost to live a Spirit-filled life as I serve God in this congregation. I will seek to fellowship daily with God through prayer, worship and Bible study. I will pray daily for the Pastors and other leadership of the church as well as for my own

area of service. I will further maintain my daily life and conduct in a manner that will be consistent with Scriptural principles of Godliness.

In The Area Of My Relationships:

I understand that God gives His church leaders. While God is my ultimate authority, I will also recognize and accept the authority of the leadership within the church including that of the pastors, spiritual leaders and other ministry leaders. In all of my relationships within the church, I will do my best to follow the admonition of Ephesians 5:21: *Submit to one another out of love for Christ.*

In The Area Of My Communication:

I recognize that as a servant in the church, the way in which I communicate both in the church and in my daily life will have a powerful effect on the lives of those around me. With that in mind, I will do my best to avoid the sins of the tongue mentioned in Scripture (Galatians 5, Colossians 3, 1 Timothy 6). As God helps me, my communication to others will reflect those things that serve to edify the church.

In The Area Of My Service:

I will approach my service in this church as a servant of Jesus Christ. The Apostle Paul said, "For though I am free from all men, I have made myself a servant to all, that I might win the more;" (1 Corinthians 9:19) I, too, desire to serve people for the cause of Christ. In my serving, I recognize that whatever ministry I may have is a gift from God and will act as a good steward of my responsibilities.

As one who serves in ministry at my church, I agree to adhere to its Constitution and Bylaws. God being my helper, I will walk in love and unity with my fellow servants.

CHAPTER 4

Altar Ministry Guidelines

Pre-Service:

The Altar Ministry Team will meet with the Team Leader fifteen minutes prior to church service for prayer and possible special instructions. Each team member should take several Follow-up Cards and other handout literature with them to the worship service.

(Altar Ministry Team members should have meeting/prayer completed ten minutes prior to the beginning of church service.)

Service:

The Altar Ministry Team should continue in an attitude of prayer during church service, asking God to specifically use each member in a special way during their time of ministry at the altar. All should come with an attitude of service-giving, not receiving.

Altar Ministry Call:

Generally, at the close of church service, the Altar Ministry team will be instructed by the Senior Pastor to come to the front of the sanctuary. Each member should pay close attention to the Pastor while making his/her way to the altar area, as the Pastor may give special instructions for the Altar Ministry Team. Unless otherwise directed, each Altar Ministry Team member should stand facing the congregation. If individuals needing ministry are already at the altar, Altar Ministry Team members should respect-fully walk around them so that a Team Member is looking at each altar respondent face-to-face. The following guidelines will greatly assist each Altar Ministry Team member in providing the most effec-tive ministry at the altar.

- Be brief with introductory remarks while encouraging the altar respondent to be concise as well. ("How may I pray for you today?") If the individual requests salvation or rededica-tion, lead them. If they want prayer, then pray for them. <u>The most important thing that can be offered at the altar is prayer, not wise counsel.</u> See the section in this book entitled "Praying With Someone At The Altar" for more infor-mation on providing direction in prayer
- Pray with the altar respondent, always pointing them to Jesus

- Complete a follow-up card for each individual/ couple that is ministered to at the altar. If you are aware of a specific need that can possibly be addressed by one of the ministries of the church, please indicate this on the follow-up card
- When prayer is finished with the altar respondent, look to see if anyone else is still in need of ministry at the altar

Post-Service:

After the Altar Ministry Team members have concluded their ministry at the altar, they should give the completed Follow-up Cards to the Altar Ministry Team Leader. Contact the individual(s) that were prayed with at the altar call within the next day or two and let each one know that you are continuing to pray for them. Emphasize that they are welcome to go to the altar for prayer at any time and that they are an important part of the family of God and the church.

CHAPTER 5

Praying With Someone at the Altar

Determining Need:

The best possible way for an Altar Ministry Worker to determine the need of the respondent to an altar call is to ask them what their need is. This can be accomplished by making a brief statement to the respondent, encouraging a concise response from the individual(s). An example of this would be to say, "Tell me in a sentence or two how I can pray for you today." Be careful not to get into a discussion of the individual's personal issues. The role of the Altar Ministry Worker is not to provide counseling, but to guide in prayer and direction for ongoing ministry. If given long explanations, the Altar Ministry Worker may need to gently interrupt and say, "OK, let's pray."

Occasionally, someone will respond to the Altar Call because of a perceived need or issue need or issue in their life, while God wants to touch them in a different area.

For example, an individual may say they need peace in their home when, in reality, they need to surrender their life to Christ. **Do not hesitate to ask the individual if they know Christ as their Savior.**

Praying For Salvation:

One of the great blessings of Altar Ministry is the privilege of assisting someone in the prayer of Salvation. When an individual indicates a desire to commit their life to Christ, an Altar Ministry Worker can help the individual to understand the meaning and value of the decision they are making. It is suggested that each Altar Ministry Worker do the following:

Clarify – Say something like: "You desire to confess you are a sinner and want to acknowledge God's gift of Jesus, accepting Him as Lord and Savior, is that correct?"

Pray - Lead in a simple prayer of salvation, having the individual repeat what you say. Repentance is a wonderful part of salvation. At its root, repent means to change direction. It is not about tears, although tears may be in order. Repentance is about a change in the person's life by turning their back on sin and embracing Jesus and the values as outlined in the Bible. Be sensitive to the respondent, listen with your heart and always assure them that Godly sorrow brings repentance and repentance means change of direction in life.

<u>Acknowledgment</u> – Encourage this new believer, reminding them of God's love and faithfulness, and that He has answered their prayer

<u>Encouragement Prayer</u> – Pray a brief prayer of encouragement, that God will guide and direct this new Christian

Assure the individual of his/her salvation using Romans 10:9. Lead the individual to make a public profession, and encourage him/her to be faithful in attendance at church, faithful to read the Word, worship and pray.

<u>Follow-up</u> – The key to the new believer growing in the faith is timely follow-up and connection to a group that can provide support and nurturing.

- Fill out the Follow-up Card (make sure you can read all information given)
- Inform the individual you will call them in the next few days to follow-up
- Make sure the individual has a Bible
- Give the individual the New Believer literature. Show the individual where to start reading in the New Testament to grow in their new-found faith

- Turn in the Follow-up Card to the Altar Ministry Team Leader or Ministry Director

Suggested Salvation Scriptures

Locate the Scriptures that you want to use in your Bible. It is almost always better to have the individual read the Scripture aloud. Do not force this, but encourage them to do so. You do not need to use every Scripture every time.

John 3:3 *Most assuredly, I say to you, unless one is born again, he cannot see the kingdom of God.*

John 3:5 *Most assuredly, I say to you, unless one is born of water and the Spirit, he cannot enter the kingdom of God.*

John 3:7 *Do not marvel that I said to you, 'You must be born again'.*

Matt. 18:3 *...Assuredly, I say to you, unless you are converted and become as little children, you will by no means enter the kingdom of heaven.*

Luke 13:3 *I tell you, no; but unless you repent you will all likewise perish.*

John 1:12 *But as many as received Him, to them He gave the right to become children of God, to those who believe in His name.*

John 5:24 *Most assuredly, I say to you, he who hears My word and believes in Him who sent Me has everlasting life, and shall not come into judgment, but has passed from death into life.*

John 6:37 *All that the Father gives Me will come to Me, and the one who comes to Me I will by no means cast out.*

Romans 10:9-10 *That if you confess with your mouth the Lord Jesus and believe in your heart that God has raised Him from the dead, you will be saved.*

Ephesians 2:8-9 *For by grace you have been saved through faith, and that not of yourselves; it is the gift of God, not of works, lest anyone should boast.*

1 John 1:9 *If we confess our sins, He is faithful and just to forgive us our sins and to cleanse us from all unrighteousness.*

1 John 5:11-12 *And this is the testimony: that God has given us eternal life, and this life is in His Son. He who has the Son has life; he who does not have the Son of God does not have life.*

John 10:9 *I am the door. If anyone enters by Me, he will be saved, and will go in and out and find pasture.*

John 14:6 *Jesus said to him: I am the way, the truth, and the life. No one comes to the Father except through Me.*

2 Corinthians 5:17 *Therefore, if anyone is in Christ, he is a new creation; old things have passed away; behold, all things have become new.*

John 3:16 *For God so loved the world that He gave His only begotten Son, that whoever believes in Him should not perish but have everlasting life.*

Romans 6:23 *For the wages of sin is death, but the gift of God is eternal life in Christ Jesus our Lord.*

Romans Road To Salvation

Romans 3:23 *For all have sinned, and fall short of the glory of God.*

Romans 6:23 *For the wages of sin is death, but the gift of God is eternal life in Christ Jesus our Lord.*

Romans 5:8 *But God demonstrates His own love toward us, in that while we were still sinners, Christ died for us.*

Romans 10:9 *That if you confess with your mouth the Lord Jesus and believe in your heart that God has raised Him from the dead, you will be saved.*

Praying For Repentance & Rededication

Some who come to the altar area are returning to church and to a relationship with Christ after a time of drifting away. They are seeking to reconnect with God after allowing their relationship with Him to falter or "back-slide." They are confessing that they are out of fellowship with God and are asking God for forgiveness, and once again acknowledging Jesus as Lord of their life.

A guideline to help in your time of ministry with this individual may go something like this:

Clarify – You may say something like: "You desire to confess that your desire is to rededicate your life to Christ, is that correct?"

Pray – Lead the individual in a simple prayer of rededication, having the individual repeat what you say.

Acknowledgment – Encourage the individual, reminding them of God's faithfulness and that He has answered their prayer.

Encouragement Prayer – Pray a brief prayer of encouragement that God will strengthen and guide them as they continue to seek Him.

Follow-up – The key to the assisting this person in their spiritual development and helping them to not turn away from the faith again is timely follow-up and connection to a group that can provide support and nurturing.

- Fill out the Follow-up Card (make sure that you can read all information)
- Inform the individual that you will call him/her in the next few days to follow-up
- Give the individual the New Believer information (*see Appendix A of this book*)
- Make sure the individual has a Bible
- Show the individual where to start reading in the New Testament to grow in their new commitment to Christ
- Ask the individual if they are involved in any area in your church. If not, encourage each person to join a group in your church such as a men's group, women's group, etc. If they are already involved in any area of your church, make a note of this on the Follow-up Card
- Turn in the Follow-up Card to the Altar Team Leader or Altar Ministry Director

Repentance and Rededication Scriptures

To Lead a Soul to Christ

John 3:3 *Jesus answered and said to him, 'Most assuredly, I say to you, unless one is born again, he cannot see the kingdom of God.'*

Romans 3:23 *For all have sinned and fall short of the glory of God.*

Romans 10:9-10 *That if you confess with your mouth the Lord Jesus and believe in your heart that God has raised Him from the dead, you will be saved. For with the heart one believes unto righteousness, and with the mouth confession is made unto salvation.*

1 John 1:9 *If we confess our sins, He is faithful and just to forgive us our sins and to cleanse us from all unrighteousness.*

Rededication

Hebrews 13:5 *Let your conduct be without covetousness; be content with such things as you have. For He Himself has said, 'I will never leave you nor forsake you.'*

Romans 5:20 *Moreover the law entered that the offense might abound. But where sin abounded, grace abounded much more.*

Matthew 18:22 *Jesus said to him, 'I do not say to you, up to seven times, but up to seventy times seven.'*

Romans 5:10 *For if when we were enemies we were reconciled to God through the death of His Son, much more, having been reconciled, we shall be saved by His life.*

Romans 8:1 *There is therefore now no condemnation to those who are in Christ Jesus, who do not walk according to the flesh, but according to the Spirit.*

Hebrews 4:15-16 *For we do not have a High Priest who cannot sympathize with our weaknesses, but was in all points tempted as we are, yet without sin. Let us therefore come boldly to the throne of grace, that we may obtain mercy and find grace to help in time of need.*

To Know For Sure

1 John 1:9 *If we confess our sins, He is faithful and just to forgive us our sins and to cleanse us from all unrighteousness.*

1 Peter 1:23 *Having been born again, not of corruptible seed but incorruptible, through the word of God which lives and abides forever.*

Romans 8:2 *For the law of the Spirit of life in Christ Jesus has made me free from the law of sin and death.*

John 8:36 *Therefore if the Son makes you free, you shall be free indeed.*

1 Corinthians 3:17 *If anyone defiles the temple of God, God will destroy him. For the temple of God is holy, which temple you are.*

Praying For Salvation

Six Steps to Salvation*

Men still cry, "What must I do to be saved?"
The Bible provides a clear answer.

1. **Acknowledge** *For all have sinned and fall short of the glory of God* (Romans 3:23). *God, be merciful to me a sinner!* (Luke 18:13).
2. **Repent** *I tell you, no; but unless you repent you will all likewise perish.* (Luke 13:3). *Repent therefore and be converted, that your sins may be blotted out, so that times of refreshing may come from the presence of the Lord* (Acts 3:19).
3. **Confess** *If we confess our sins, He is faithful and just to forgive us our sins, and to cleanse us from all unrighteousness* (1 John 1:9). *That if you confess with your mouth the Lord Jesus and believe in your heart that God has raised Him from the dead, you will be saved.* (Romans 10:9).
4. **Forsake** *Let the wicked forsake his way, and the unrighteous man his thoughts; Let him return to the Lord, and He will have mercy on him; and to our God, for He will abundantly pardon.* (Isaiah 55:7)

5. **Believe** *For God so loved the world that He gave His only begotten Son, that whoever believes in Him should not perish but have everlasting life.* (John 3:16). *He who believes and is baptized will be saved; but he who does not believe will be condemned.* (Mark 16:16).

6. **Receive** *He came to His own, and His own did not receive Him. But as many as received Him, to them he gave the right to become children of God, to those who believe in His name.* (John 1:11-12).

* From Full Gospel Businesmen's Fellowship International

Praying For Salvation

The Pathway to Life with Jesus Christ

John 3:3-10 *Jesus answered and said to him, 'Most assuredly, I say to you, unless one is born again, he cannot see the kingdom of God.' Nicodemus said to Him, 'How can a man be born when he is old? Can he enter a second time into his mother's womb and be born?' Jesus answered, 'Most assuredly, I say to you, unless one is born of water and the Spirit, he cannot enter the kingdom of God. That which is born of the flesh is flesh, and that which is born of the Spirit is spirit. Do not marvel that I said to you, 'You must be born again,' The wind blows where it wishes, and you hear the sound of it, but cannot tell where it comes from and where it goes. So is everyone who is born of the Spirit.' Nicodemus answered and said to Him, 'How can these things be?' Jesus answered and said to him, 'Are you the teacher of Israel, and do not know these things?'*

Romans 10:8-10 *But what does it say? 'The word is near you, in your mouth and in your heart' (that is, the word of faith which we preach): that if you confess with your mouth the Lord Jesus and believe in your heart that God has raised Him from the dead, you will be saved. For with the heart one believes unto righteousness, and with the mouth confession is made unto salvation.*

John 1:12 *But as many as received Him, to them He gave the right to become children of God, to those who believe in His name.*

Ephesians 2:8-9 *For by grace you have been saved through faith, and that not of yourselves; it is the gift of God, not of works, lest anyone should boast.*

2 Corinthians 5:17 *Therefore if anyone is in Christ, he is a new creation; old things have passed away; behold, all things have become new.*

Colossians 3:10 *And have put on the new man who is renewed in knowledge according to the image of Him who created him.*

Colossians 1:12-14 *Giving thanks to the Father who has qualified us to be partakers of the inheritance of the saints in the light. He has delivered us from the power of darkness and conveyed us into the kingdom of the Son of His love, in whom we have redemption through His blood, the forgiveness of sins.*

John 8:36 *Therefore if the Son makes you free, you shall be free indeed.*

Romans 8:2 *For the law of the Spirit of life in Christ Jesus has made me free from the law of sin and death.*

1 John 1:7-10 *But if we walk in the light as He is in the light, we have fellowship with one another, and the blood of Jesus Christ His Son cleanses us from all sin. If we say that we have no sin, we deceive ourselves, and the truth is not in us. If we confess our sins, He is faithful and just to forgive us our sins and to cleanse us from all unrighteousness. If we say that we have not sinned, we make Him a liar, and His word is not in us.*

1 John 5:13 *These things I have written to you who believe in the name of the Son of God, that you may know that you have eternal life, and that you may continue to believe in the name of the Son of God.*

Scriptures for Skeptics

THE CHRISTIAN WORKERS' TEXT*

Scriptures to use with those individuals who give the following reasons for not becoming born again:

a. Not today.

Joshua 24:15 - Choose you this day.
1 Kings 18:21 - How long halt ye?
Proverbs 27:1 - Boast not thyself of tomorrow.
Isaiah 55:6 - While he may be found.
Matthew 24:44 - In such an hour as ye think not.
Luke 12:19, 20 - Thou fool.
Acts 22:16 - Now why tarriest thou?
2 Corinthians 6:2 - Now is the accepted time.

b. It is too late.

Ezekiel 33:19 - If the wicked turn…he shall live.
Matthew 20:6 - Why stand ye here all the day idle?
John 6:37 - Him that cometh unto me.
Romans 10:13 - Whosoever shall call upon the name of the Lord.

c. Tried once and Failed.

God is able:
—To deliver. Daniel 3:17

—To fulfill promises. Romans 4:21
—To guard your treasure. 2 Timothy 1:12
—To save to the uttermost. Hebrews 7:25
—To keep you from falling. Jude 24

d. Too Many Mysteries.
Deuteronomy 29:29 - The secret things belong to God.
John13:7 - Thou shalt know hereafter.
Acts 1:7 - It is not for you to know.
1 Co.13:12 - Now we see through a glass, darkly.

e. I don't need a Saviour.
John 3:18 - He that believeth not is condemned already.
John 3:36 - He that believeth not...the wrath of God abideth on him.
Romans 3:23 - All have sinned.
Romans 6:23 - The wages of sin is death.
Hebrews 2:3 - How shall we escape, if we neglect?

f. If God is love, there is no Danger.
Matthew 22:13 - Cast him into outer darkness.
Luke 13:3 - Except ye repent, ye shall all likewise perish.
2 Peter 2:4 - If God spared not the angels.

g. Too Many Hypocrites in the Church.

Job 8:13 - The hypocrite's hope shall perish.

Matthew 7:1 - Judge not, that ye be not judged.

Romans 14:12 - Everyone of us shall give an account of himself.

1 Peter 4:8 - Above all things have fervent charity among yourselves.

h. It Will Cost Me Too Much.

Psalms 116:12 - What shall I render unto the Lord?

Mark 8:36 - What shall it profit?

Luke 18:29-30 - No man hath left...who shall not receive more.

1 Peter 2:24 - Who...bare our sins in his own body on the tree.

i. I Cannot Leave my Old Companions.

Exodus 23:2 - Thou shalt not follow a multitude to do evil.

Proverbs 13:20 - He that walketh with wise men, shall be wise.

2 Corinthians 6:14 - Be ye not unequally yoked together with unbelievers.

1 Corinthians 15:33 - Be not deceived...evil communications corrupt.

j. I Shall Be Persecuted.

Matthew 5:11 - There is a blessing connected with it.

Matthew 5:12 - It lifts the soul to the plane of the prophets.

2 Timothy 3:12 - All godly people expect it...

Revelation 2:10 - It leads to a crown.

* Used by permission B. B. Kirkbride Bible Co. Inc.

CHAPTER 6

Water Baptism

It is the right of every new Christian in the New Testament to indicate that he/she is committing himself or herself fully to Jesus Christ. By going into the baptismal water, believers visibly demonstrate their faith before the Christian community and to the world.

1. Water baptism into Christ (Galatians 3:27) signifies that one now is the property of Christ and has a share in:
   a. His life
   b. His spirit
   c. His inheritance

Galatians 3:26-4:7 *For you are all sons of God through faith in Christ Jesus. For as many of you as were baptized into Christ have put on Christ. There is neither Jew nor Greek, there is neither slave nor free, there is neither male nor female; for you are all one in Christ Jesus. And if you are Christ's, then you are Abraham's seed, and heirs according to the promise. Now I say that the heir, as long as he is a child, does not differ at all from a slave, though he is master of all, but is under guardians and stewards until the time appointed by the father. Even so we, when we were children, were in bondage under the elements of the world. But when the fullness of the time had come, God sent forth His Son, born of a woman, born under the law, to redeem those who were under the law, that we might receive the adoption as sons. And because you are sons, God has sent forth the Spirit of His Son into your hearts, crying out, 'Abba, Father!'*

Romans 8:14-17 *For as many as are led by the Spirit of God, these are sons of God. For you did not receive the spirit of bondage again to fear, but you received the Spirit of adoption by whom we cry out, 'Abba, Father.' The Spirit Himself bears witness with our spirit that we are children of God, and if children, then heirs – heirs of God and joint heirs with Christ, if indeed we suffer with Him, that we may also be glorified together.*

2. Water baptism is a response to what Christ has done for the believer. To be valid, it must be
   a. Preceded by repentance
   b. A personal faith in Jesus Christ

Colossians 2:12 *Buried with Him in baptism, in which you also were raised with Him through faith in the working of God, who raised Him from the dead.*

3. If one has a sincere heart of faith and commitment to Jesus as Lord and Savior, then one outwardly acknowledges the receipt of grace given to us by the Father Himself.

4. Water baptism is an outward sign and testimony of our receiving Christ as Lord and Savior and of the washing away of sins.

Titus 3:5 *Not by works of righteousness which we have done, but according to His mercy He saved us, through the washing of regeneration and renewing of the Holy Spirit.*

1 Peter 3:21 *There is also an antitype which now saves us-baptism (not the removal of the filth of the flesh, but the answer of a good conscience toward God), through the resurrection of Jesus Christ.*

Acts 2:38 *Then Peter said to them, 'Repent, and let every one of you be baptized in the name of Jesus Christ for the remission of sins; and you shall receive the gift of the Holy Spirit.'*

5. Water baptism portrays the union of the believer with Christ in His death, burial and resurrection. This signifies an end to the life of sin and the beginning of a new life in Christ. The following scriptures may be used to provide a better understanding of water baptism.

Romans 6:1-11 *What shall we say then? Shall we continue in sin that grace may abound? Certainly not! How shall we who died to sin live any longer in it? Or do you now know that as many of us as were baptized into Christ Jesus were baptized into His death? Therefore we were buried with Him through baptism into death, that just as Christ was raised from the dead by the glory of the Father, even so we also should walk in newness of life. For if we have been united together in the likeness of His death, certainly we also shall be in the likeness of His resurrection, knowing this, that our old man was crucified with Him, that the body of sin might be done away with, that we should no longer be slaves of sin. For he who has died has been freed from sin. Now if we died with Christ, we believe that we shall also live with Him, knowing that Christ, having been raised from the dead, dies no* more. *Death no longer has dominated over Him. For the death that He died, He died to sin once for all; but the life that He lives, He lives to God. Likewise you also, reckon yourselves to be dead indeed to sin, but alive to God in Christ Jesus our Lord.*

Colossians 2:11-12 *In Him you were also circumcised with the circumcision made without hands, by putting off the body of the sins of the flesh, by the circumcision of Christ, buried with Him in baptism, in which you also were raised with Him through faith in the working of God, who raised Him from the dead.*

Romans 6:3-4, 7, 10, 12 *Or do you not know that as many of us as were baptized into Christ Jesus were baptized into His death? Therefore we were buried with Him through baptism into death, that just as Christ was raised from the dead by the glory of the Father, even so we also should walk in newness of life. For he who has died has been freed from sin. For the death that He died, He died to sin once and for all; but the life that He lives, He lives to God. Therefore do not let sin reign in your mortal body, that you should obey it in its lusts.*

Colossians 3:3-17 *For you died, and your life is hidden with Christ in God. When Christ who is our life appears, then you also will appear with Him in glory. Therefore put to death your members which are on the earth: fornication, uncleanness, passion, evil desire, and covetousness, which is idolatry. Because of these things the wrath of God is coming upon the sons of disobedience, in which you yourselves once walked when you lived in them. But now you yourselves are to put off all these: anger, wrath, malice, blasphemy, filthy language out of your mouth. Do not lie to one another, since you have put off the old man with his deeds, and have put on the new man who is renewed in knowledge according to the image of Him who created him, where there is neither Greek nor Jew, circumcised nor uncircumcised, barbarian, Scythian, slave nor free, but Christ is all and in all. Therefore, as the elect of God, holy and beloved, put on tender mercies, kindness, humility, meekness, longsuffering; bearing one with one another, and forgiving one another, if anyone has a complaint against another; even as Christ forgave you, so you also must do. But above all these things put on love, which is the bond of perfection. And let the peace of God rule in your hearts, to which also you were called in one body; and be thankful. Let the word of Christ dwell in you richly in all wisdom, teaching and admonishing one another in psalms and hymns and spiritual songs, singing with grace in your hearts to the Lord.*

And whatever you do in word or deed, do all in the name of the Lord Jesus, giving thanks to God the Father through Him.

Colossians 2:12-13 *Buried with Him in baptism, in which you also were raised with Him through faith in the working of God, who raised Him from the dead. And you, being dead in your trespasses and the uncircumcision of your flesh, He has made alive together with Him, having forgiven you all trespasses.*

Therefore, water baptism involves a commitment to a lifelong practice of turning one's back on the world and all that is evil (Romans 6:5-6, 11-13) and living a new life in the sprit that reflects God's standards of righteousness.

Romans 6:5-6, 11-13 *For if we have been united together in the likeness of His death, certainly we also shall be in the likeness of His resurrection, knowing this, that our old man was crucified with Him, that the body of sin might be done away with, that we should no longer be slaves of sin...Likewise you also, reckon yourselves to be dead indeed to sin, but alive to God in Christ Jesus our Lord. Therefore do not let sin reign in your mortal body, that you should obey it in its lusts. And do not present your members as instruments of unrighteousness to sin, but present your-*

selves to God as being alive from the dead, and your members as instruments of righteousness to God.

CHAPTER 7

The Baptism in the Holy Spirit

About the Baptism in the Holy Spirit

The Power of Pentecost is a promise for all who accept Christ as Lord. The opportunity to pray with someone for the Baptism in the Holy Spirit is a joy for every Altar Minister. Some principles to keep in mind when praying with someone for the Baptism in the Holy Spirit are:

FAITH – We do not earn our salvation, neither do we earn the baptism in the Holy Spirit. This is a gift that, like salvation, is received by faith. The seeker ought not to be holding on to any sin if he wants to be baptized in the Spirit. But, at the same time, he does not have to do anything or attain a certain level of maturity before he may be baptized. He simply needs to ask and believe and allow. "Allow" will be explained later in this book.

FULLNESS – Every believer has the Holy Spirit residing within him. That residence began at salvation. The baptism in the Holy Spirit is an immersion into the Spirit which will bring a greater power to do the will of God to the believer's life.

GIFT – The gift that seeker is seeking is the Holy Spirit; speaking in tongues is the result of receiving that gift. We receive this baptism by faith, by asking the Lord for this gift and by believing that we receive the gift.

EVIDENCE – Speaking in tongues is not the same as the infilling; it is an evidence of the infilling. Christians in the Book of Acts were convinced that other believers had been filled when it was known that they spoke in tongues. We consider tongues to be the initial, physical evidence of the infilling. This implies that there are other evidences that will follow in the experience of the baptized believer. Therefore, when the seeker speaks in tongues, this is not an indication that he has arrived at the highest plateau. It is, rather, an indication that he has been filled with this Spirit and is now ready to embark on a Spirit-controlled life. While speaking in tongues is not the ultimate goal, neither is it unimportant. The Book of Acts indicates that speaking in tongues is standard procedure for those who are baptized in the Spirit. Indeed, it indicates that the believer truly has been immersed in the Spirit, for if the Lord has the tongue, then He has the whole person.

ALLOW – As the seeker asks God in faith to be filled with the Holy Spirit, he should focus his attention on the Lord Jesus and worship Him verbally. As he does so, he will probably begin to feel an unusual sensation within him. Many times, people will dismiss this as a feeling that has been self-induced. However, the Christian who is asking in faith for the blessing of the Lord can be sure that this feeling is from God. He should set aside the doubt and cooperate with this unusual sensation. By that, we mean that the seeker ought to put questions on hold, forge ahead in his worship of Jesus, and allow whatever it is that is in the person's spirit to be expressed verbally.

To Be Filled with the Holy Spirit

When you meet a person at the altar who is born again and indicates a desire to be filled with the Holy Spirit, you do not need to do a lot of teaching or elaborate explanation. Some might ask about the benefit of being filled with the Holy Spirit. Some might think they received it all at salvation. To be sure, the individual that is born again has the Holy Spirit residing within. The baptism with/in the Holy Spirit is a different dimension, a deeper, fuller walk with Jesus Christ through the Holy Spirit.

When we are baptized in/with the Holy Spirit, the Holy Spirit is allowed to live through us more fully. Acts 1:8 says, "But you shall receive power when the Holy Spirit has come upon you; and you shall be witnesses to Me in Jerusalem, and in all Judea and Samaria, and to the end of the earth." When we are filled/baptized with/in the Holy Spirit, we hear the voice of the Lord more clearly and in greater depth. Yes, we heard the call of the Spirit when we were born again and now He wants to take us deeper in our relationship with Him.

The only requirements for receiving the baptism of the Holy Spirit are:

1. You must be born again, saved, received Jesus Christ into your life.
2. You must ask. Luke 11:11-13 *If a son asks for bread from any father among you, will he give him a stone? Or if he asks for a fish, will he give him a serpent instead of a fish? Or if he asks for an egg, will he offer him a scorpion? If you then, being evil, know how to give good gifts to your children, how much more will your heavenly Father give the Holy Spirit to those who ask Him!*
3. You must believe.
4. You must receive.

There are, however, a few things to keep in mind:

Clarify – Ask if the person has been born again. If the answer is yes, then say, "You desire to receive the gift of the Baptism in the Holy Spirit, is that correct?"

<u>Pray</u> – Pray a simple prayer of encouragement, asking God to give the wonderful gift of the Holy Spirit, and evidence thereof.

<u>Give Direction</u> – The Altar Ministry Worker is to give the following direction to the individual: "In your own words, asks the Lord to fill you with His Holy Spirit, believe that God will do that for you, worship Jesus out loud, and allow yourself to speak whatever God puts into your spirit. As you do that, I am going to lay my hands on you and ask the Lord to fill you as well." In some churches, the laying on of hands is not practiced. It is not absolutely necessary to have hands laid upon an individual to receive the Holy Spirit, but there is a transference of this anointing and it is generally easier for the individual to receive.

When the person is ready to pray and ask the Lord to fill them with the Holy Spirit, agree with their prayer. As you pray, you should be exercising your own faith, worshipping Jesus, and praying in tongues if you feel led to do so. It is proper to encourage the timid with exhortations such as "Go ahead; let it out" or "Let your tongue speak what you feel in your heart." No one can be filled with the Holy Spirit with their mouths closed.

If, after a few minutes, the seeker does not seem to be getting anywhere, you might want to start over. You might even ask if there seems to be a hindrance to the Spirit's work or if there is any unconfessed sin in the person's life. If so, take care of that right away through repentance.

If you have run out of time and the person has not been filled, then encourage the individual to keep believing for this gift throughout the week. Tell the individual that you would like to meet him/her back at the altar the following Sunday, whether the individual has been filled with the Spirit during the week or not. Assure the individual that they shall receive as promised in Luke 11:11-13. Then get out the Follow-Up Card and fill out the information. Go through the referral process of making sure the person is a part of your ministry, i.e., men's group, women's group, etc. Assure this person that you will be praying for him/her throughout the week.

Encouragement Prayer – Pray a brief prayer of encouragement that God will strengthen and guide each person as they continue to seek Him.

Follow-up – The key to assisting each person in their spiritual development is timely follow-up and connection to a group within your ministry that can provide support.

- Fill out the Follow-up Card
- Turn in the Follow-up Card to the Altar Ministry Team Leader or Altar Minister Director

Holy Spirit Baptism Scriptures

But you will receive power when the Holy Spirit has come upon you; and you shall be witnesses to Me in Jerusalem, and in all Judea and Samaria, and to the end of the earth. Acts 1:8

And they were all filled with the Holy Sprit and began to speak with other tongues, as the Spirit gave them utterance. Acts 2:4

Then Peter said to them, 'Repent and let every one of you be baptized in the name of Jesus Christ for the remission of sins; and you shall receive the gift of the Holy Spirit. For the promise is to you and to your children, and to all who are afar off, as many as the Lord our God will call'. Acts 2:38,39

And he said to them, 'Into what then were you baptized?' So they said, 'Into John's baptism.' Then Paul said, "John indeed baptized with a baptism of repentance, saying to the people that they should believe on Him who would come after him, that is, on Christ Jesus.' When they heard this, they were baptized in the name of the Lord Jesus. And when Paul had laid hands on them, the Holy Spirit came upon them, and they spoke with tongues and prophesied. Now the men were about twelve in all. Acts 19:3-7

PRAYER: One possible prayer for asking to be filled with the Holy Spirit:

Heavenly Father, thank you for sending your Son, Jesus to earth to provide the gift of our salvation.

Jesus, you promised another gift of the Holy Spirit, so I ask you, Lord Jesus, to baptize me with the Holy Spirit right now exactly like on the day of Pentecost. Thank you, Jesus. You have done your part. Now I am going to do my part. I am going to begin to praise You, Lord Jesus, but not in any language I know because I can't speak two languages at one time. I surrender myself to you fully. Have your way in my life from this time for the rest of my earthly life. In Jesus' name, I pray. Amen.

CHAPTER 8

Praying For Healing

Some who come to the altar are in need of a healing from God. Divine healing is an integral part of the Gospel. Deliverance from sickness is provided for in the atonement, and healing is a privilege of all believers.

Jesus went to the cross and shed His blood for our salvation. He gave His body for our healing. Jesus went about preaching, teaching and healing. Matthew 4:23. He sent His disciples to do the same. Matthew 10:5-8.

He also sends us to do the same. Matthew 28:19-20.

It is His will that we walk in divine health.

Matthew 7:16-17 *You will know them by their fruits. Do men gather grapes from thorn-bushes or figs from thistles? Even so, every good tree bears good fruit, but a bad tree bears bad fruit.*

Your time of ministry with the individual in need of healing may go something like this:

<u>Clarify</u> – "You desire a healing touch from God, is that correct?"

<u>Request</u> – "What specifically may I pray for?"

<u>Pray</u> – Pray a simple prayer, asking God to respond to the altar respondent's faith and release His healing touch.

<u>Encouragement</u> – Encourage the individual, reminding him/her of God's faithfulness and that He has already answered their prayer by dying on the cross for all of our sins, sickness and diseases. Possibly share some of the healing scriptures (see Appendix D) found later in this book.

Remind each individual that it is God's will to heal them.

Manifestations

Ministry at the altar is truly a supernatural experience. It is the meeting of God with man. As such, there are elements of this ministry that are profoundly God and things also occur that are human emotion.

The role of the altar team member in the midst of it all is to minister to the altar call respondent.

People respond differently to the presence of the Holy Spirit. Some will become quite emotional, others will be quiet and reflective, and some may display physical manifestations as the power of God comes upon them. These manifestations should come as no surprise to the individual familiar with the power of Pentecost.

The goal is to minimize the issues that would keep people <u>from</u> receiving effective ministry from the Holy Spirit. There are occasions when it will be necessary for some of the altar ministry team to serve in a support capacity, assisting people who are physically overcome by the power of God (commonly referred to as "slain in the spirit") to the floor. Modesty blankets should be available to cover anyone who might be in a potentially compromising position. Women should <u>always</u> cover women.

It is the responsibility of the Pastor to respond to potential excess at the altar. All Altar Ministry Workers should be sensitive to and respond to the Pastor's instruction.

The possibility of physical manifestations is one of several reasons we very strongly encourage Altar Ministry Workers to pray with altar respondents of their own gender. It is our desire to prevent any concerns of impropriety at the altar.

Physical manifestations are not suggested or encouraged to altar call respondents, and the altar team member is cautioned not to allow their own emotions to overtake the working of the Holy Spirit. In essence, let God be God at the altar.

Faith & Healing Scriptures

I have fought the good fight, I have finished the race, I have kept the faith. 2 Timothy 4:7

But without faith it is impossible to please Him, for he who comes to God must believe that He is, and that He is a rewarder of those who diligently seek Him. Hebrews 11:6

That is, that I may be encouraged together with you by the mutual faith both of you and me. Romans 1:12

Examine yourselves as to whether you are in the faith. Test yourselves. Do you not know yourselves, that Jesus Christ is in you?-unless indeed you are disqualified. 2 Corinthians 13:5

My brethren, count it all joy when you fall into various trials, knowing that the testing of your faith produces patience. James 1:2-3

And said, 'If you diligently heed the voice of the Lord your God and do what is right in His sight, give ear to His cammandments, and keep all His statutes, I will put none of the diseases on you which I have brought on the Egyptians. For I am the Lord who heals you. Exodus 15:26

The Lord will strengthen him on his bed of illness; You will sustain him on his sickbed. Psalm 41:3

And the Lord will take away from you all sickness, and will afflict you with none of the terrible diseases of Egypt which you have known, but will lay them on all those who hate you. Deuteronomy 7:15

But he was wounded for our transgressions, He was bruised for our iniquities; the chastisement for our peace was upon Him, and by His stripes we are healed. Isaiah 53:5

We live by faith, not by sight. 2 Corinthians 5:7

Is anyone among you sick? Let him call for the elders of the church, and let them pray over him, anointing him with oil in the name of the Lord. James 5:14

Who forgives all your iniquities, who heals all your diseases. Psalm 103:3

Who Himself bore our sins in His own body on the tree, that we, having died to sins, might live for righteousness—by whose stripes you were healed. 1 Peter 2:24

APPENDIX A

SUGGESTED NEW BELIEVER INFORMATION/ALTAR RESPONDENT LETTER FROM SENIOR PASTOR

Dear New Believer:

Congratulations on your commitment to Jesus Christ! You have just made the most important decision that you will ever make in your life—accepting Jesus Christ as your Lord and Savior. At this point, you may have some questions about being a born-again Christian. This information will help answer those questions and guide you in your journey toward the Kingdom of God.

While your physical body will die someday, your spirit is the part of you that will live forever. However, the Bible says that our souls and spirits are dead and dark because of original human sin. And,

God cannot stay in the presence of sin. The *only* way to remove that darkness and sin is to become "born again". When you were born again, you became a "new creature" in Christ Jesus. This means that your old moral and spiritual condition completely passed away and you were given an opportunity for a new beginning with Christ Jesus. This "new birth" is possible because God loves you so much that He sent His only Son to die in your place for your sins. Because of Jesus' sacrifice, you are no longer blind, lost or living in darkness.

Jesus is the Way, the Truth and the Life. There is no other way to peace and happiness. However, salvation is not mental; it is of the heart. When you are truly born again, there is something in you that will cause you to be different. Your goals, motives, attitudes and actions will begin to change. While this does not mean that you will never make mistakes again, it does mean that you will not purposely or knowingly continue to sin.

God's Word is truth and life to your spirit. Your spirit needs to be fed and nourished, so it is very important that you become part of and regularly attend a Bible-believing church that is filled with the power of the Holy Spirit, where the power of God is in action—to feed the Spirit of God that is in the new you. We, (*insert your church name here*), would be honored if you joined us for Sunday services. It is also important for you to learn God's Word by reading the Bible on a regular basis. We recommend the New King James, the New American Standard, the New International or the Contemporary Versions of the Bible. Start by reading the Book of John, proceed to the Book of Matthew and then read the entire New Testament. It is also important that you receive sound, spiritual teaching. We encourage you to become a part of (*your church name*). Attend regularly. You will find friends here.

God is always with you, so praying to God in Jesus' name and talking to God will help bring you closer into His presence. Singing songs of praise to God and participating in fellowship with other Christians will help bring you closer into the presence of God as well. We are here to help you. We will answer questions and point you in the right direction. Please talk to any one of our Pastoral staff or call our office.

Without regard to your past, you are welcome at (*insert the name of your church here*). Welcome to the family of God!

APPENDIX B

FOLLOW-UP CARD

CHURCH NAME
Pastor's Name
Altar Counselors Information Card

NAME: _____

ADDRESS: _____

CITY: _____ STATE: _____ ZIP: _____

TELEPHONE: _____

____SALVATION ____ REDEDICATION ____ ASSURANCE OF SALVATION

____ HEALING ____ PERSONAL ISSUES

OTHER _____

DATE _____ ALTAR COUNSELOR _____

APPENDIX C

ETERNAL LIFE SCRIPTURES

ETERNAL LIFE

1. Why is the question, "Have you been born again?" life's most important question? John 3:3,7; Romans 8:9

   John 3:3, 7 *Jesus answered and said to him, 'Most assuredly, I say to you, unless one is born again, he cannot see the kingdom of God.' 'Do not marvel that I said to you, 'You must be born again.'*

   Romans 8:9 *But you are not in the flesh but in the Spirit, if indeed the Spirit of God dwells in you. Now if anyone does not have the Spirit of Christ, he is not His.*

2. Why did God send Jesus into the World? John 3:16-17

   John 3:16-17 *'For God so loved the world that He gave His only begotten Son, that whoever believes in Him should not perish but have everlasting life. For God did not send His Son into the world to condemn the world, but that the world through Him might be saved.'*

3. What is eternal life? What does eternal mean? John 17:3

   John 17:3 *'And this is eternal life, that they may know You, the only true God, and Jesus Christ whom You have sent.'*

4. Why did Jesus say He came into the world? Luke 19:10, John 10:10

   Luke 19:10 *'For the Son of Man has come to seek and to save that which was lost.'*

   John 10:10 *'The thief does not come except to steal, and to kill, and to destroy. I have come that they may have life, and that they may have it more abundantly.'*

5. How do I know He loves me enough to save me? John 3:16, Romans 5:8

John 3:16 '*For God so loved the world that He gave His only begotten Son, that whoever believes in Him should not perish but have everlasting life.*'

Romans 5:8 '*But God demonstrates His own love toward us, in that while we were still sinners, Christ died for us.*'

6. How do I get Jesus to come into my life? John 1:12

John 1:12 '*But as many as received Him, to them He gave the right to become children of God, to those who believe in His name.*'

7. What is the difference in receiving Jesus into my life and just knowing about Him? 2 Corinthians 5:17

2 Corinthians 5:17 '*Therefore, if anyone is in Christ, he is a new creation; old things have passed away; behold, all things have become new*'

8. What has happened because I have confessed that Jesus is my Savior and the Son of God? 1 John 4:14-15

1 John 4:14-15 '*And we have seen and testify that the Father has sent the Son as Savior of the world. Whoever confesses that Jesus is*

the Son of God, God abides in him, and he
in God.'

9. Can I know for certain that I have Christ living
   inside me? How? 1 John 3:24; 1 John 5:7, 10

   1 John 3:24 *'Now he who keeps His command-
   ments abides in Him, and He in him. And by
   this we know that He abides in us, by the
   Spirit whom He has given us.'*

   1 John 5:7, 10 *'For there are three that bear
   witness in heaven: The Father, the Word,
   and the Holy Spirit; and these three are one.
   He who believes in the Son of God has the
   witness in himself; he who does not believe
   God has made Him a liar, because he has not
   believed the testimony that God has given of
   His Son.'*

10. In what way does the Holy Spirit assure me that
    I am a child of God? Romans 8:16

    Romans 8:16 *'The Spirit Himself bears
    witness with our spirit that we are children
    of God.'*

11. What is one of the basic reasons God inspired the
    letter of First John to be written? 1 John 5:13

    1 John 5:13 *'These things I have written to
    you who believe in the name of the Son of*

God, that you may know that you have eternal life, and that you may continue to believe in the name of the Son of God.'

12. What did Paul say about his assurance of salvation? 2 Timothy 1:12

    2 Timothy 1:12 *'For this reason I also suffer these things; nevertheless I am not ashamed, for I know whom I have believed and am persuaded that He is able to keep what I have committed to Him until that Day.'*

13. What does Christ guarantee to those in whom He comes to live? John 1: 28-29

    John 1:28-29 *These things were done in Bethabara beyond the Jordan, where John was baptizing. The next day John saw Jesus coming toward him and said, 'Behold! The Lamb of God who takes away the sin of the world!'*

14. What can separate me from the love of God which is in Christ? Romans 8:35-39

    Romans 8:35-39 *'Who shall separate us from the love of Christ? Shall tribulation, or distress, or persecution, or famine, or nakedness, or peril, or sword? As it is written: 'For your sake we are killed all day long; we are accounted as sheep for the slaughter.'*

Yet in all these things we are more than conquerors through Him who loved us. For I am persuaded that neither death nor life, nor angels nor principalities nor powers, nor things present nor things to come, nor height nor depth, nor any other created thing, shall be able to separate us from the love of God which is in Christ Jesus our Lord.'

15. Paul knew that Christ actually lived in Him. What did he discover about how he was to experience the Christian life? Galatians 2:20

Galatians 2:20 *I have been crucified with Christ; it is no longer I who live, but Christ lives in me; and the life which I now live in the flesh I live by faith in the Son of God, who loved me and gave Himself for me.*

16. How should I behave now that Christ lives in me? Romans 12:1-2, 9-13

'I beseech you therefore, brethren, by the mercies of God, that you present your bodies a living sacrifice, holy, acceptable to God, which is your reasonable service. And do not be conformed to this world, but be transformed by the renewing of your mind, that you may prove what is good and acceptable and perfect will of God.'
Let love be without hypocrisy. Abhor what is evil. Cling to what is good. Be kindly affectionate to one another with brotherly love, in

honor giving preference to one another; not lagging in diligence, fervent in spirit, serving the Lord; rejoicing in hope, patient in tribulation, continuing steadfastly in prayer; distributing to the needs of the saints, given to hospitality.

17. What should characterize my life? Mark 12:30-31

Mark 12:30-31 *'And you shall love the Lord your God with all you heart, with all your soul, with all your mind, and with all your strength.' This is the first commandment. And the second, like it, is this: 'You shall love your neighbor as yourself.' There is no other commandment greater than these.'*

18. How can I show the Lord Jesus I love Him? John 14:21, 23

John 14:21, 23 *'He who has My command-ments and keeps them, it is he who loves Me. And he who loves Me will be loved by My Father, and I will love him and manifest Myself to him.'...Jesus answered and said to him, 'If anyone loves Me, he will keep My word; and My Father will love him, and We will come to him and make Our home with him.'*

19. What are some of the ways that I can show others that I love them? Romans 12:10-21

Romans 12:10-21 *'Be kindly affectionate to one another with brotherly love, in honor giving preference to one another; not lagging in diligence, fervent in spirit, serving the Lord; rejoicing in hope, patient in tribulation, continuing steadfastly in prayer; distributing to the needs of the saints, given to hospitality. Bless those who persecute you; bless and do not curse. Rejoice with those who rejoice, and weep with those who weep. Be of the same mind toward one another. Do not set your mind on high things, but associate with the humble. Do not be wise in your own opinion. Repay no one evil for evil. Have regard for good things in the sight of all men. If it is possible, as much as depends on you, live peaceably with all men. Beloved, do not avenge yourselves, but rather give place to wrath; for it is written, 'Vengeance is Mine, I will repay,' says the Lord. Therefore 'if your enemy is hungry, feed him; if he is thirsty, give him a drink; for in so doing you will heap coals of fire on his head.' Do not be overcome by evil, but overcome evil with good.'*

20. What has God faithfully promised if I seek, above everything else, His lordship over my life? Matthew 6:33

    Matthew 6:33 *'But seek first the kingdom of God and His righteousness, and all these things shall be added to you.'*

21. Of what did Christ warn me to beware? Luke 12:15 Why?

    Luke 12:15 *'And He said to them, 'Take heed and beware of covetousness, for one's life does not consist in the abundance of the things he possesses.'*

22. What will happen if I use my life for my own selfishness and do not give it in service to God and man? John 12:25-26

    John 12:25-26 *'He who loves his life will lose it, and he who hates his life in this world will keep it for eternal life. If anyone serves Me, let him follow Me; and where I am, there My servant will be also. If anyone serves Me, him My Father will honor.'*

23. How do I know that I am a child of God and Christ lives within me?
    2 Corinthians 5:17

    2 Corinthians 5:17 *'Therefore, if anyone is in Christ, he is a new creation; old things have passed away; behold, all things have become new.'*

APPENDIX D

HEALING SCRIPTURES

HEALING FOR THE BODY

These Scriptures are your medicine and must be taken every day. As you read these Scriptures ALOUD, faith rises in your heart to believe, and your faith touches the power of God that is present to heal.

Meditate and personalize them; the Holy Spirit will make some scriptures come alive to you, and they will be what you should think about between readings.

...For I am the Lord who heals you. Exodus 15:26

...And I will take sickness away from the midst of you. Exodus 23:25

And the Lord will take away from you all sickness... Deuteronomy 7:15

No evil shall befall you, Nor shall any plague come near your dwelling. Psalms 91:10

Because he has set his love upon Me, therefore I will deliver him; I will set him on high, because He has known My name. He shall call upon Me, and I will answer Him; I will be with Him in trouble; I will deliver him and honor him. With long life I will satisfy him, And show him My salvation. Psalms 91:14-16

Bless the LORD, O my soul; and all that is within me, bless His holy name! Bless the Lord, O my soul, and forget not all His benefits: who forgives all your iniquities, who heals all your diseases, who redeems your life from destruction, who crowns you with loving-kindness and tender mercies, who satisfies your mouth with good things, so that your youth is renewed like the eagle's. Psalms 103:1-5

Their soul abhorred all manner of food; and they drew near to the gates of death. Then they cried out to the LORD in their trouble, and He saved them out of their distresses. He sent His word and healed them, and delivered them from their destructions. Oh, that men would give thanks to the LORD for His goodness, and for His wonderful works to the children of men! Let them sacrifice the sacrifices of thanksgiving, and declare His works with rejoicing. Psalms 107:18-22

I shall not die, but live, and declare the works of the Lord. Psalms 118:17

My son, give attention to my words; incline your ear to my sayings. Do not let them depart from your eyes; keep them in the midst of your heart; for they are life to those who find them, and health to all their flesh. Keep your heart with all diligence, for out of it spring the issues of life. Put away from you a deceitful mouth, and put perverse lips far from you. Proverbs 4:20-24

Fear not, for I am with you; be not dismayed, for I am your God. I will strengthen you, yes, I will help you, I will uphold you with My righteous right hand. Isaiah 41:10

Surely He has borne our griefs and carried our sorrows; yet we esteemed Him stricken, smitten by God, and afflicted. But He was wounded for our transgressions, He was bruised for our iniquities; the chastisement for our peace was upon Him, and by His stripes we are healed. Isaiah 53:4-5

Then the Lord said to me, 'You have seen well, for I am ready to perform My word.' Jeremiah 1:12

'For I will restore health to you and heal you of your wounds', says the LORD.... Jeremiah 30:17

...Let the weak say, 'I am strong.' Joel 3:10

What do you conspire against the Lord? He will make an utter end of it. Affliction will not rise up a second time. Nahum 1:9

But to you who fear My name the Sun of Righteousness shall arise with healing on His wings; and you shall go out and grow fat like stall-fed calves. Malachi 4:2

And behold, a leper came and worshiped Him, saying, 'Lord, if You are willing, You can make me clean.' Then Jesus put out His hand and touched him, saying, 'I am willing; be cleansed'... Matthew 8:2-3

'Assuredly, I say to you, whatever you bind on earth will be bound in heaven, and whatever you loose on earth will be loosed in heaven. Again I say to you that if two of you agree on earth concerning anything that they ask, it will be done for them by My Father in heaven. For where two or three are gathered together in My name, I am there in the midst of them.' Matthew 18:18-20

(Prayer of agreement-bind on earth what is bound in heaven: sickness, disease, infirmities; loose on earth what is loosed in heaven: healing and health for spirit, soul and body.)

So Jesus answered and said to them, 'Assuredly, I say to you, if you have faith and do not doubt, ...but also if you say to this mountain, 'Be removed and be case into the sea,' it will be done. And whatever things you ask in prayer, believing, YOU WILL RECEIVE.' (*Emphasis supplied*). Matthew 21:21-22.

For assuredly, I say to you, whoever says to this mountain, 'Be removed and be cast into the sea,' and does not doubt in his heart, but believes that those things he says will be done, he will have whatever he says. Therefore I say to you, whatever things you ask when you pray, believe that you receive them, and you will have them. And whenever you stand praying, if you have anything against anyone, forgive him, that your Father in heaven may also forgive you your trespasses. But if you do not forgive, neither will your Father in heaven forgive your trespasses. Mark 11:23-26

So Jesus answered and said to them, 'Have faith in God.' Mark 11:22

And these signs will follow those who believe: In My name they will case out demons; they will speak with new tongues; they will take up serpents; and if they drink anything deadly, it will by no means hurt them; they will lay hands on the sick, and they will recover. Mark 16:17-18

...Jesus the Christ heals you... Acts 9:34

And not being weak in faith, he did not consider his own body, already dead (since he was about a hundred years old), and the deadness of Sarah's womb. He did not waver at the promise of God through unbelief, but was strengthened in faith, giving glory to God, and being fully convinced that what He had promised He was also able to perform. Romans 4:19-21

For the law of the Spirit of life in Christ Jesus has made me free from the law of sin and death. Romans 8:2

But if the Spirit of Him who raised Jesus from the dead dwells in you, He who raised Christ from the dead will also give life to your mortal bodies through His Spirit who dwells in you. Romans 8:11

For though we walk in the flesh, we do not war according to the flesh. For the weapons of our warfare are not carnal but mighty in God for pulling down strongholds, casting down arguments and every high thing that exalts itself against the knowledge of God, bringing every thought into captivity to the obedience of Christ. 2 Corinthians 10:3-5

Cast down thoughts of fear, and of what you see or hear in the natural that is contrary to God's healing Truth.

Christ has redeemed us from the curse of the law, having become a curse for us (for it is written, 'Cursed is everyone who hangs on a tree.') Galatians 3:13

Finally, my brothers, be strong in the Lord and in the power of His might. Put on the whole armor of God, that you may be able to stand against the wiles of the devil. For we do not wrestle against flesh and blood, but against principalities, against powers, against the rulers of the darkness of this age, against spiritual hosts of wickedness in the heavenly places. Therefore take up the whole armor of God, that you may be able to withstand in the evil day, and having done all, to stand. Stand therefore, having girded your waist with truth, having put on the breastplate of righteousness, and having shod your feet with the preparation of the gospel of peace; above all, taking the shield of faith with which you will be able to quench all the fiery darts of the wicked one. And take the helmet of salvation, and the sword of the Spirit, which is the word of God; praying always with all prayer and supplication in the Spirit, being watchful to this end with all perseverance and supplication for all the saints- Ephesians. 6:10-18

For it is God who works in you both to will and to do for His good pleasure. Philippians 2:13

It is His will and His good pleasure to heal me! Praise be to my merciful God and His loving kindness and His Presence in me, doing what needs to be done to make me whole!

Be anxious for nothing, but in everything by prayer and supplication, with thanksgiving, let your requests be made known to God; and the peace of God, which surpasses all understanding, will guard your hearts and minds through Christ Jesus. Finally, brethren, whatever things are true, whatever things are noble, whatever things are just, whatever things are pure, whatever things are lovely, whatever things are of good report, if there is any virtue and if there is anything praiseworthy-meditate on these things. Philippians 4:6-8

For God has not given us a spirit of fear, but of power and of love and of a sound mind. 2 Timothy 1:7

Let us hold fast the confession of our hope without wavering, for He who promised is faithful. Hebrews 10:23

Therefore do not cast away your confidence, which has great reward. For you have need of endurance, so that after you have done the will of God, you may receive the promise. Hebrews 10:35-36

By faith Sarah herself also received strength to conceive seed, and she bore a child when she was past the age, because she judged Him faithful who had promised. Hebrews 11:11

Jesus Christ is the same yesterday, today, and forever. Hebrews 13:8

Is anyone among you sick? Let him call for the elders of the church, and let them pray over him, anointing him with oil in the name of the Lord. And the prayer of faith will save the sick, and the Lord will raise him up. And if he has committed sins, he will be forgiven. James 5:14-15

Confess your trespasses to one another, and pray for one another, that you may be healed. The effective, fervent prayer of a righteous man avails much. James 5:16

When evening had come, they brought to Him many who were demon-possessed. And He cast out the spirits with a word, and healed all who were sick, that it might be fulfilled which was spoken by Isaiah the prophet, saying: 'He Himself took our infirmities and bore our sicknesses.' Matthew 8:16-17

Who Himself bore our sins in His own body on the tree, that we, having died to sins, might live for righteousness-by whose stripes you were healed. 1 Peter 2:24

Beloved, if our heart does not condemn us, we have confidence toward God. And whatever we ask we receive from Him, because we keep His commandments and do those things that are pleasing in His sight. And this is His commandment: that we should believe on the name of His Son Jesus Christ and love one another, as He gave us commandment. 1 John 3:21-23

Now this is the confidence that we have in Him, that if we ask anything according to His will, He hears us. And if we know that He hears us, whatever we ask, we know that we have the petitions that we have asked of Him. 1 John 5:14-15

'Ah, Lord God! Behold, You have made the heavens and the earth by Your great power and outstretched arm. There is nothing too hard for You...' *'Behold, I am the Lord, the God of all flesh. Is there anything too hard for Me?'* Jeremiah 32:17, 27

For with God nothing will be impossible...But He said, 'The things which are impossible with men are possible with God.' Luke 1:37, 18:27

But Jesus looked at them and said, 'With men it is impossible, but not with God; for with God all things are possible.' Mark 10:27

Jesus said to him, 'If you can believe, all things are possible to him who believes.' Mark 9:23

Set your mind on things above, not on things on the earth. Colossians 3:2

So Jesus said to them, 'Because of your unbelief; for assuredly, I say to you, if you have faith as a mustard seed, you will say to this mountain, 'Move from here to there,' and it will move; and nothing will be impossible for you.' Matthew 17:20

But when Jesus heard it, He answered him, saying, 'Do not be afraid; only believe, and she will be made well.' Luke 8:50

And He said to her, 'Daughter, be of good cheer; your faith has made you well. Go in peace.' Luke 8:48

"So ought not this woman, being a daughter of Abraham, whom Satan has bound-think of it-for eighteen years, be loosed from this bond on the Sabbath?" Luke 13:16

Then I said, 'Behold, I have come-In the volume of the book it is written of Me-To do Your will, O God.' Hebrews 10:7

How God anointed Jesus of Nazareth with the Holy Spirit and with power, who went about doing good and healing all who were oppressed by the devil, for God was with Him. Acts 10:38

Your kingdom come. Your will be done on earth as it is in heaven. Matthew 6:10 There is no sickness, pain or disease in heaven.

Fight the good fight of faith... 1 Timothy 6:12

For to be carnally minded is death, but to be spiritually minded is life and peace. Romans 8:6

Isaiah 53—This whole chapter tells how Jesus provided righteousness for your spirit, peace for your soul, healing for your body.

Your healing <u>begins</u> in your spirit or heart, as the Holy Spirit makes the Word of God TRUTH, <u>alive</u> in you. Then it spreads to your body in manifestation of the healing. Speaking these truths aloud casts out the fear, doubt and unbelief that hinders healing. FAITH comes by hearing.

Altar Ministry Worker Commitment Form

The following commitment form should be signed by each person who desires to be an Altar Ministry Worker following a training class.

MY COMMITMENT

1. I will pray faithfully for the Pastor, the leadership team, the members of the Altar Ministry Team and the church body.
2. I am committed to [insert your church name here] and the established ministry goals.
3. I will be faithful in attending church on a regular basis.
4. I will be diligent to prepare myself to serve prior to each church service. (Spending time in the Word and praying on a daily basis.)
5. I am a tither. I will give the first tenth of all my income to [insert your church name here] in obedience to the Lord and as a reminder that I belong to the Lord Jesus Christ.
6. I am committed to winning the lost to Jesus Christ.
7. I regard myself as being a member of a ministry team. If I see a special problem, I will help if I can or I will notify those in leadership who are qualified to minister to that need.
8. I will reach out promptly to those who are absent or hurting.

9. I will be regular in my personal and family devotions to keep my heart and house in order and my focus on the things of God.

10. I am eager to receive training and instruction. I trust God to build my character and skills through the insights of those He has placed over me in this ministry.

11. When misunderstandings or interpersonal conflicts arise, I will go to the person with whom I have a problem and privately and quickly make every effort to restore a good relationship (keep strife far from you). (You may also go to the Senior Pastor or Associate Pastor in these situations.)

12. I purpose to avoid being any part of gossip or backbiting, either as a listener or a giver of negative talk about a fellow believer. (This type of activity will nullify your prayer life... this includes refraining from talking about the things people bring to you for prayer.)

13. I am committed to growing in the pursuit of excellence in my work for the Lord. I will seek training when I have the opportunity, and will be the best I can be at my assigned tasks.

_____   _____

Signed by   Date

<u>Altar Workers Training Certification Form</u>

I have attended the Altar Ministry Workers training session and understand the responsibilities and privileges involved in this duty. I feel I would be an asset to the Altar Ministry team and I am willing to learn and offer my services to my church.

Applicant's Name:_____ Date: _____

Date:_____

Approval of Altar Minister Director: _____

Approval of Senior Pastor: _____

CPSIA information can be obtained at www.ICGtesting.com
Printed in the USA
LVOW100009160911

246409LV00001B/60/P